PREMIER EDITION
MEDITATION
MAGAZINE
AF489229
RENITY NOW
LEARN TO GAIN
CONTROL OF THE
THE MOST
POWERFUL TOOL
YOU HAVE......
YOUR MIND
LISA DELORES

≫ Table of Contents

6 — The Power of Thought to Create a Life You Love, Empower, are Passionate about with Purpose
By Lisa Delores

9 — Understanding how we create with our thoughts

18 — The Emotional Benefit of Meditation

20 — The power of Words & Imagery

21 — Sweetness Redefined: Exploring Healthier Alternatives to Sugar
by PAULETTE HENSON

27 — Mandala Adult Coloring

44 — Discovering You - About Lisa Delores

Email:lisa@lisadelores.com

Paulette Henson

Editor's Note

Editor-in-Chief

Dear Readers,

Welcome to the latest issue of Mindful Magazine, a collaboration born from a shared vision to empower individuals on their journey towards self-discovery and inner peace. As the Editor-in-Chief, I am thrilled to share with you the profound impact that meditation and mindfulness, guided by certified Meditation & Wellness Coach Lisa Schmidt, have had on my life, and how this collaboration came to fruition.

My journey into the world of meditation began when I had the privilege of meeting Lisa Schmidt—an encounter that would change the trajectory of my life. Under Lisa's compassionate guidance, I experienced meditation for the first time —an experience that left me profoundly transformed.

As I settled into a comfortable posture and closed my eyes, I was enveloped by a sense of tranquility and serenity. With each breath, I felt the stresses of daily life melt away, replaced by a profound sense of peace and inner stillness. It was a moment of revelation—a glimpse into the transformative power of mindfulness and meditation.

Inspired by my experience, I embarked on a journey of self-discovery and exploration, guided by Lisa's wisdom and expertise. Together, we collaborated to create Mindful Magazine—a platform dedicated to supporting Lisa's vision and mission to empower individuals to help themselves through the practice of meditation and mindfulness.

Each issue of Mindful Magazine is crafted with the intention of providing you, our cherished readers, with the tools, insights, and inspiration you need to embark on your own journey of self-discovery and inner peace. Through articles, interviews, and guided practices, we invite you to join us as we explore the transformative power of mindfulness and meditation and their profound impact on our lives.

As you journey through the pages of this magazine, I encourage you to open your heart and mind to the possibilities that lie within. May you find solace, inspiration, and empowerment in these pages, and may they serve as a guiding light on your path towards a life of mindfulness, joy, and fulfillment.

With gratitude and mindfulness,

PAULETTE HENSON
Editor-in-Chief Mindful Magazine

MINDFULNESS FOR MENTAL HEALTH

Cultivating Awareness and Inner Peace

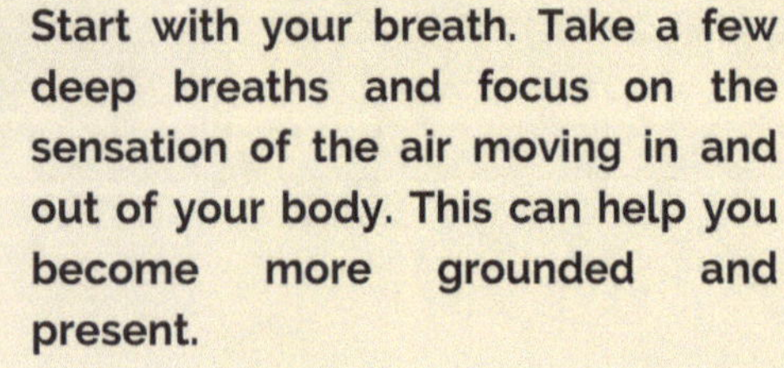

Mindfulness is the practice of being present and aware in the moment. It can help reduce stress and anxiety, improve mood, and promote overall well-being. Here are some tips to help you cultivate mindfulness.

Start with your breath. Take a few deep breaths and focus on the sensation of the air moving in and out of your body. This can help you become more grounded and present.

Practice mindful meditation. Set aside a few minutes each day to sit in quiet reflection. Focus on your breath, body sensations, or a mantra to help you stay present.

Engage your senses. Take a few moments to notice the sights, sounds, smells, and tastes around you. Engaging your senses can help bring you into the present moment.

MEDITATION

for beginners
by

Lisa Delores

The Power of Thought to Create a Life You Love, Empowered, Passionate, & on Purpose
By Lisa Delores

By now most of us have heard that our thoughts create our reality. The Buddha said that 2,600 years ago. How could something said so long ago still be relevant today? And what does that really mean? Isn't reality, reality? Don't we all live in the same reality? Actually, no, we do not all live in the same reality!   We all live in our own version of reality. This is even more apparent today as we get our news and information from our phones and computers where algorithms feed us information that fits our world view, severely limiting new ideas and viewpoints

Two people can witness the same event and when questioned about that event they often tell quite different stories. How can that be? Didn't they see the same thing?   That can be because the world you live in reflects your thoughts, your values, and your beliefs. Your thoughts, values, and beliefs come from your family, your church, your education, your community, the city in which you live.   Our beliefs become our thoughts, our thoughts become our actions, and our actions create our world...the friends you choose, the car you drive, the clothes you wear, and where you choose to spend your time.

Everything we see around us was first created in the mind of someone...cars, buildings, homes, clothes, art, airplanes, everything! Everything in your life came from your mind. Therefore, our thoughts create our world. And that puts YOU in the driver seat of your life because you are in charge of your thoughts. But we are not taught that in school. We are not taught that we control our minds. We are not taught how to control our thoughts, so we end up thinking and allowing our thoughts to control us or allowing someone else to tell us what to think. So, when you change your mind, you change your world.

The world you live in reflects your energy, focus, and beliefs. This means that you are in control of the world you live in. And if you do not like what you have created, the apartment, the job, the car, then you have the power to change it. That is great news! But how exactly do you do that? To create a new life, you must think new thoughts. Below are the three first steps to help you create new thoughts, live empowered, and create the life you desire.

1. AWARENESS

Awareness is the first step to transformation. Being aware that you have the power to control your thoughts puts you in control. Start noticing your thoughts. What are you thinking about when you are driving? What are you thinking about when you are taking a shower, cooking dinner, or eating lunch? What are you thinking about when your boss or coworker is talking to you? Being aware of what you are thinking brings you into the present moment where your power is. If you are thinking about the past or the future you are thinking about things that do not exist and that will create anxiety, stress, and frustration. Being fully present with your thoughts allows you to be in control and make decisions from your heart.

2. UNDERSTANDING

Understanding that you are in control of your mind allows you to take control of your life. If you are not in control of your thoughts then who is? Your parents, your spouse, advertisers? When you accept that you are in control of your mind you are no longer the victim of circumstance. You can change your mind, change your thoughts, and therefore change your life.

.3. PRACTICE

Once you accept that you are in control you then have the power to create change in your life. But this will not happen overnight. Just like the life you have now did not emerge overnight, it is years in the making. It will take time to change your old habits, patterns, and beliefs. It will take practice and dedication and you will make mistakes. But that is ok! Be gentle with yourself and allow yourself the space to grow. Meditation is a powerful practice to teach you how to notice your thoughts and not get triggered by them. There are a lot of meditation teachers, apps, and schools. Take some time to try a few out and find the one that works for you. Remember that this will take time and be easy with yourself. Just like going to the gym to change your body may take a month or two to see results, meditation is the "gym" for your mind and it may take a few months to get in the groove and see results. You are a powerful creator! Now what is that you want to create? Thoughts create, so chose from your heart!

UNDERSTANDING HOW WE CREATE WITH OUR THOUGHTS

Living a passionate, fulfilled life on purpose is possible! How do we that?

HERE'S A STEP-BY-STEP TO GET STARTED WITH AN INTENTIONAL PRACTICE:

- Get clear on what you desire (the end result)

- Write it down in detail

- In meditation visualize you living your desire

- Feel the feelings in that moment of manifesting your desire

- Believe the Universe will bring it to you

- Expect your desire to become a reality

A PEEK INSIDE MY MIND

In these clouds, write down all of your thoughts and feelings that are having. They can be happy thoughts, sad thoughts, worried thoughts, excited thoughts!

Fold along the dotted line so the two stars touch.

Thoughts are Things

Watch your thoughts for they become words,

Watch your words for they become actions,

Watch your actions for they become habits,

Watch your habits for they become your character,

Watch your character for it becomes your destiny.

-Ralph Waldo Emerson

The thought manifest as word,
The word manifest as the deed,
The deed develops into habit,
And the habit hardens into character.
So watch the thoughts and its way with care,
And let it spring from love born out of concern for all beings.

-Buddha

meditation:
the practice of harnessing the power of your mind

do more
OF WHAT YOU LOVE.

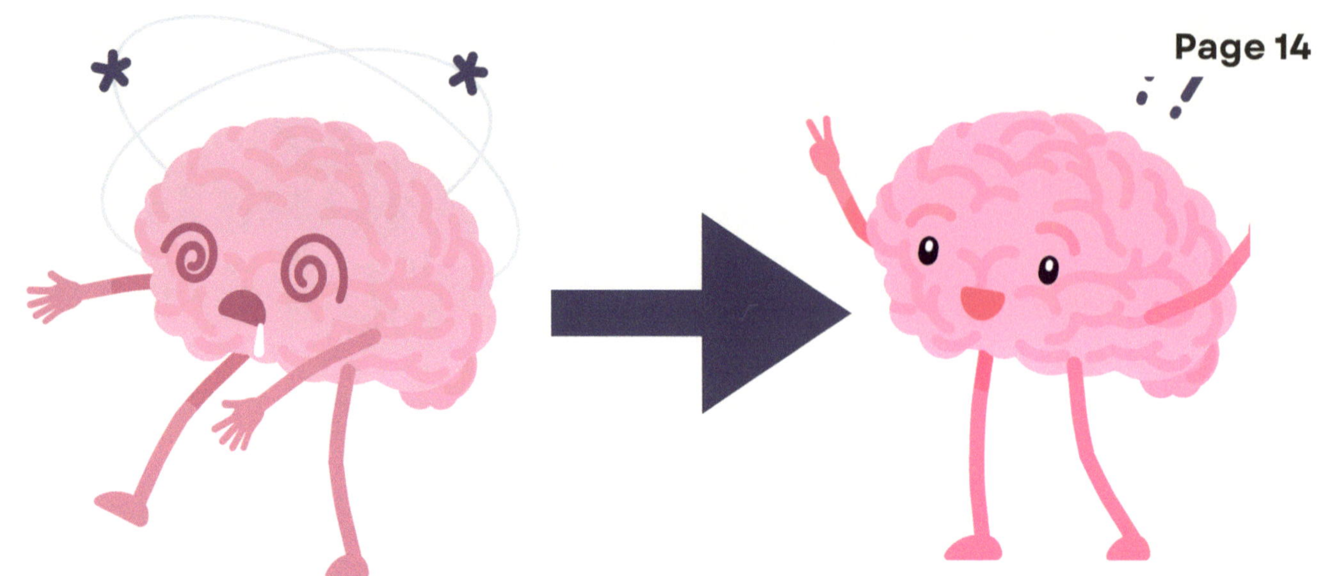

DEVELOPING EMOTIONAL INTELLIGENCE

Understand Yourself and Others

Recognize your emotions to better understand what you feel and why

Develop the ability for empathy and compassion to deeply understand other people

Emotional intelligence will help improve your relationships and communication with others

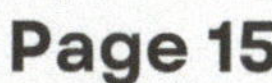

Remember This!
Be kind to
your mind

learning how to be mindful

THE BENEFITS OF YOGA

Yoga improves strength, balance, and flexibility. Give more energy and brighter moods.

LIVING YOUR YOGA

Balance on one foot while holding the other leg to your calf or above the knee (but never on the knee) at a right angle. Try to focus on one spot in front of you. While you balance for one minute.

You may feel increased mental and physical energy, a boost in alertness and enthusiasm, and fewer negative feelings after getting into a routine of practicing yoga.

THE EMOTIONAL BENEFIT OF

Meditation

Building skills to manage your stress

Increasing self-awareness

Increasing patience & tolerance

Reducing negative emotions

Focusing on the present

Increasing imagination & creativity

Meditation offers a sanctuary from the relentless pace of modern life, providing numerous mental health benefits. One of the most profound advantages is the reduction of stress and anxiety. Through regular practice, meditation helps calm the mind, allowing individuals to step back from their daily worries and find a sense of inner peace. By focusing on the present moment, practitioners can break free from the cycle of rumination and worry, significantly lowering their stress levels and improving overall mental well-being.

In addition to its stress-reducing properties, meditation enhances cognitive functions such as focus and concentration. By training the mind to sustain attention on a single point of focus, whether it be the breath, a mantra, or a visual object, meditation strengthens the brain's ability to maintain concentration. This improvement in focus not only boosts productivity but also enhances problem-solving skills and creativity. Over time, consistent meditation practice can lead to better decision-making and increased mental clarity, empowering individuals to navigate their daily tasks with greater efficiency and insight.

THE POWER OF WORDS & IMAGERY

Understanding the power of how you create your life through words and images is profound. It's about harnessing the creative energy of language and visualization to shape your reality. This is how we create and we can do it intentionally or allow the whims of others... society, friends, teachers, parents or priest to dictate what we think and therefore create our lives. Words have the ability to evoke emotions, inspire action, and manifest intentions. When you combine them with images, you engage both the conscious and subconscious mind, amplifying the impact.

Think of it this way: when you consistently affirm positive statements about yourself and your goals, you're programming your subconscious mind to believe in and work toward those outcomes. Visualization is key to realizing your goals. You must be able to see your desired outcome! By creating mental images of your desired reality, reinforcing your intentions and feeling that it is done you set the wheels in motion and the Universe responds.

Through meditation, journaling, affirmations, vision boards, or creative writing the process of using words and images to create your life is about setting intentions, clarifying goals, and maintaining focus. It's a way to align your thoughts, beliefs, and actions with what your are committed to create in your life.

By practicing meditation, mindfulness, and consciously directing your thoughts and imagery towards your desired outcomes, you can cultivate a more positive mindset, increase motivation, and ultimately, bring your dreams into reality. It's not about wishful thinking but rather about intentional living and taking proactive steps towards the life you envision.

BY PAULETTE HENSON

SWEETNESS REDEFINED: EXPLORING HEALTHIER ALTERNATIVES TO SUGAR

Alternatives to Sugar!

Sugar has long been a staple ingredient in our diets, adding sweetness to our favorite treats and beverages. However, as concerns about the negative health effects of excessive sugar consumption continue to rise, many people are seeking out healthier alternatives to satisfy their sweet cravings. In this article, we'll explore some of the most popular alternatives to refined sugar and their potential health benefits.

The Problem with Refined Sugar:

Refined sugar, often found in the form of white sugar or high-fructose corn syrup, has been linked to a range of health issues, including obesity, type 2 diabetes, heart disease, and tooth decay. Its high glycemic index can cause rapid spikes and crashes in blood sugar levels, leading to energy fluctuations and cravings for more sugary foods. Additionally, refined sugar provides empty calories devoid of essential nutrients, contributing to nutrient deficiencies and weight gain when consumed in excess.

***2. Sweetness from the Earth: Maple Syrup:

Derived from the sap of maple trees, pure maple syrup is a delectable and natural sweetener. Rich in antioxidants and minerals, it adds a unique flavor profile to your dishes. Look for 100% pure maple syrup without added sugars or corn syrup for the most nutritional benefits.

**3. The Wonder of Stevia:

Stevia, a plant-derived sweetener, has gained popularity for being a calorie-free, natural alternative to sugar. Steviol glycosides, the compounds responsible for its sweetness, make stevia an excellent option for those monitoring their calorie intake or managing blood sugar levels. Experiment with stevia extracts or blends to find your preferred sweetness level.

**4. Coconut Sugar: A Sweet Essence from the Tropics:

Derived from the sap of coconut palm trees, coconut sugar is a natural sweetener with a lower glycemic index compared to traditional sugar. It provides a subtle caramel flavor and retains some of the nutrients present in the coconut sap. Use it as a 1:1 substitute in your recipes for a touch of tropical sweetness.

**5. Molasses Magic:

Blackstrap molasses, a byproduct of sugar refining, is rich in iron, calcium, and potassium. While it has a robust flavor, a little goes a long way. Use molasses to add depth to baked goods, marinades, and savory dishes. Opt for unsulfured blackstrap molasses for the most nutritional benefits.

**6. Fruitful Sweetness: Dates and Date Syrup:

Dates, nature's candy, can be blended into a paste or used as a whole-food sweetener. Date syrup, made by simmering dates in water, offers a natural sweetness that works well in various recipes. Dates also provide fiber and essential nutrients, making them a wholesome alternative to refined sugar.

**7. Monk Fruit Magic:

Monk fruit sweetener, derived from the monk fruit, is a zero-calorie sweetener that's gaining popularity. Known for its intense sweetness, monk fruit sweetener is often blended with other ingredients to balance its potency. It's a great option for those looking to reduce their sugar intake without sacrificing sweetness.

Conclusion:

As we navigate the journey towards healthier living, choosing alternatives to refined sugar allows us to savor the sweetness of life without compromising our well-being. Experiment with these natural sweeteners to discover the flavors that resonate with your taste buds. By embracing these alternatives, you not only satisfy your sweet tooth but also contribute to a more conscious and mindful approach to nutrition. Sweeten your life naturally, and let the delicious journey begin!

WHAT'S COOKING?

Three delicious recipes to add to your menu

. Quinoa and Black Bean Stuffed Peppers:

Ingredients:

- 4 large bell peppers (any color)
- 1 cup quinoa, cooked
- 1 can black beans, drained and rinsed
- 1 cup corn kernels
- 1 cup cherry tomatoes, diced
- 1 cup red onion, finely chopped
- 1 cup salsa
- 1 teaspoon cumin
- 1 teaspoon chili powder
- Salt and pepper to taste
- 1 cup shredded cheddar cheese (optional for topping)
- Fresh cilantro for garnish

Instructions:

1. Preheat the oven to 375°F (190°C).
2. Cut the tops off the bell peppers and remove seeds.
3. In a large bowl, mix together cooked quinoa, black beans, corn, cherry tomatoes, red onion, salsa, cumin, chili powder, salt, and pepper.
4. Stuff each pepper with the quinoa mixture.
5. Place the stuffed peppers in a baking dish and cover with aluminum foil.
6. Bake for 25-30 minutes until peppers are tender.
7. If desired, sprinkle shredded cheddar cheese on top during the last 5 minutes of baking.
8. Garnish with fresh cilantro before serving.

•

<u>Sweet Potato and Chickpea Curry:</u>

<u>Ingredients:</u>

- 2 large sweet potatoes, peeled and diced
- 1 can chickpeas, drained and rinsed
- 1 onion, finely chopped
- 2 cloves garlic, minced
- 1 tablespoon curry powder
- 1 teaspoon ground cumin
- 1 teaspoon ground coriander
- 1 teaspoon turmeric
- 1 can coconut milk
- 1 can diced tomatoes
- Salt and pepper to taste
- Fresh cilantro for garnish
- Cooked brown rice or quinoa for serving

<u>Instructions:</u>

- In a large pot, sauté the onion and garlic until softened.
- Add the sweet potatoes, chickpeas, curry powder, cumin, coriander, and turmeric. Stir to coat evenly.
- Pour in the coconut milk and diced tomatoes. Season with salt and pepper.
- Bring the mixture to a boil, then reduce the heat and let it simmer for 20-25 minutes or until sweet potatoes are tender.
- Serve the curry over cooked brown rice or quinoa.
- Garnish with fresh cilantro before serving.

Grilled Lemon Herb Chicken Salad:

Ingredients:

- 2 boneless, skinless chicken breasts
- 2 tablespoons olive oil
- Juice of 1 lemon
- 1 teaspoon dried oregano
- 1 teaspoon dried thyme
- Salt and pepper to taste
- Mixed salad greens (spinach, arugula,
- or your preference)
- Cherry tomatoes, halved
- Cucumber, sliced
- Red onion, thinly sliced
- Feta cheese, crumbled
- Balsamic vinaigrette dressing

Instructions:

- In a bowl, whisk together olive oil, lemon juice, oregano, thyme, salt, and pepper.
- Marinate chicken breasts in the mixture for at least 30 minutes.
- Preheat the grill or grill pan over medium-high heat.
- Grill chicken for 6-8 minutes per side or until fully cooked.
- Let the chicken rest for a few minutes, then slice it into strips.
- Assemble the salad by placing mixed greens on a plate and adding cherry tomatoes, cucumber, red onion, and grilled chicken.
- Sprinkle feta cheese on top.
- Drizzle with balsamic vinaigrette dressing before serving.

GO WITHIN

Mandala

Adult Coloring Pages

Mandala

Mandala

Mandala

Mandala

Mandala

Mandala

Mandala

Mandala

Mandala

Mandala

Mandala

Mandala

Mandala

Mandala

Thoughts that make you Successful

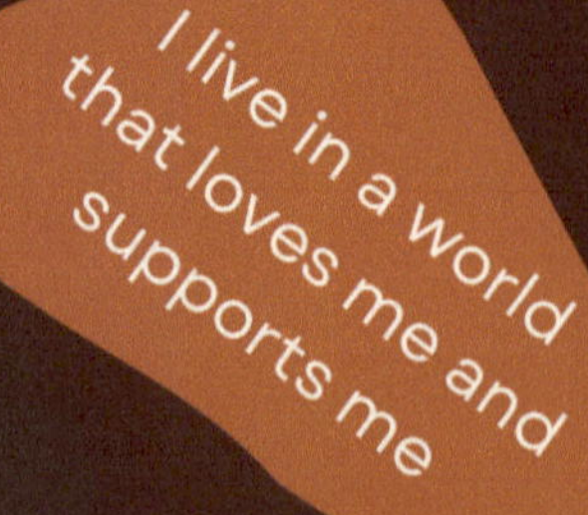

I fully and freely forgive everyone no matter what they may have said or done

I love myself therefore I create healthy boundaries with others

I love myself therefore, I speak kindly to myself

I live in a world that loves me and supports me

MEDITATION

✳

PRACTICE A FEW MINUTES OF MEDITATION OR MINDFULNESS EXERCISES TO CALM YOUR MIND AND SET A POSITIVE TONE FOR THE DAY.

Discovering the Power of Meditation: A Journey Within

In the fast-paced hustle and bustle of modern life, it's easy to get swept away by the endless demands and distractions that surround us. Caught in the whirlwind of our thoughts and emotions, we often find ourselves feeling overwhelmed, stressed, and disconnected from our innermost selves. In times like these, it's essential to pause, breathe, and turn inward—to discover the transformative power of meditation.

What is Meditation?

Meditation is a practice that involves training your mind to focus and redirect your thoughts. It is used to quiet the mind, discover inner peace, deepen self-awareness, and to connect with something greater than oneself, whether it be the divine, nature, love, or the collective consciousness. There are many types of meditation....active or passive meditation, guided meditation, walking meditation, mindfulness meditation, and many more. The specific techniques and philosophies vary, but the underlying goal remains consistent: spiritual growth and personal transformation.

Are you ready to look within and walk your personal divine path?

Through a unique blend of proven coaching methods and meditation, I guide people to discover their path and uncover their own answers. My coaching is rooted in the belief that everyone has the potential for profound transformation by access their own answers.

Contact me at 949-466-0051 or lisa@lisadelores.com

The benefits of meditation and mindfulness are vast and profound, encompassing physical, mental, emotional, and spiritual well-being. Scientific research has shown that regular meditation practice can:

- Reduce stress and anxiety: By calming the nervous system and quieting the mind, meditation helps to alleviate stress and anxiety, promoting a sense of relaxation and ease.
- Improve focus and concentration: Mindfulness meditation strengthens our ability to sustain attention and focus, enhancing productivity, creativity, and cognitive function.
- Cultivate emotional resilience: Through the practice of mindfulness, we learn to relate to our emotions with greater awareness and acceptance, reducing reactivity and fostering emotional balance.
- Enhance self-awareness and insight: Meditation encourages self-reflection and introspection, deepening our understanding of ourselves and our patterns of thought and behavior.
- Foster compassion and connection: Mindfulness cultivates a sense of empathy and kindness towards ourselves and others, fostering deeper connections and relationships.

While formal meditation practice is an essential component of mindfulness, the true power of mindfulness lies in its integration into our daily lives. Simple practices such as mindful breathing, mindful eating, and mindful walking can be incorporated into our routines, allowing us to bring awareness and presence to each moment of our day.

In a world filled with distractions and noise, mindfulness offers us a pathway to inner peace, clarity, and well-being. By cultivating a practice of mindfulness and meditation, we can awaken to the fullness of life, embracing each moment with presence, gratitude, and openness. As we journey inward, may we discover the profound wisdom and healing that awaits us in the depths of our own hearts and minds.

"
Find your inner peace through the gentle flow of each breath and movement.

Wellness

It will never be achieved until our body and mind are kept healthy at all times.

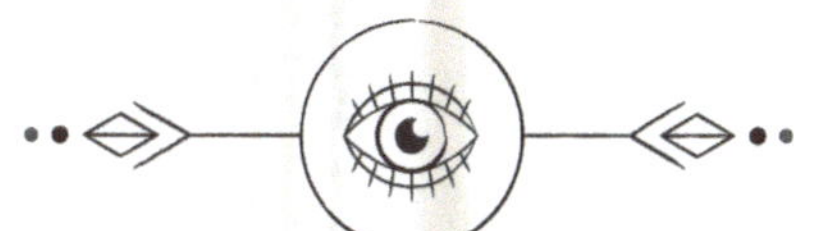

Focused in Heart.
Clear in Mind.

Schedule Your 1/1 Virtual Meditation

The Meditation Minute

Lisa Delores

email:lisa@lisadelores.com

KEEP CALM · KEEP CALM · KEEP CALM · KEEP CALM ·